HEALING

through

HOPE

Wyatt House books may be ordered through booksellers or by contacting:
WYATT HOUSE PUBLISHING
399 Lakeview Dr. W.
Mobile, Alabama 36695
www.wyattpublishing.com
editor@wyattpublishing.com

Because of the dynamic nature of the Internet, any web address or links contained in this book may have changed since publication and may no longer be valid.

Cover and interior design by: Mark Wyatt

Cover photo by Brad Sutton (brad@getthepoint.tv)

ISBN 13: 978-0-9977422-4-4

Printed in the United States of America

HEALING
through
HOPE

by
Dee Dee Graham

Wyatt House Publishing
Mobile, Alabama

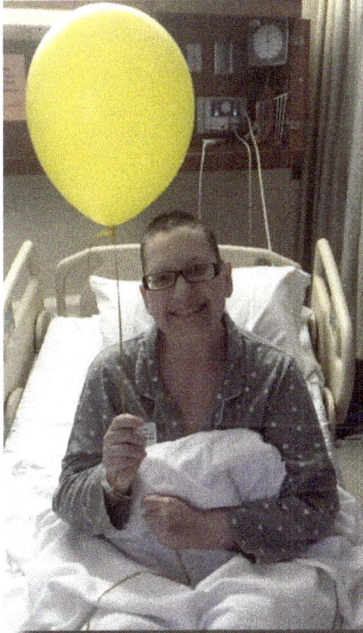

As the hospital staff normally do when someone is being discharged from rehab to go home, the day before, they will bring a yellow balloon to signify this experience. I was delighted to see the balloon for many reasons, and the most important being that to me it was a tangible sign that God had given me the hope I needed to heal me completely.

Foreword

I would like to thank the following family members and friends for your prayers, love, and support during my whole surgery process.

- To my Cottage Hill Baptist Church staff and church family. I could not have done this without your fervent prayers over all the years. And most of all to my dear friend and pastor, Dr. Alan Floyd for reading this book, giving advice and prayer, but most of all for suggesting Dr. Mark Wyatt, my publisher who has worked so hard and been so patient with me. Thank you "Uncle A" as Emily affectionately refers to him! You are a blessing to our family!

- To the Azalea City Kiwanis, Alabama District, and

the International Kiwanis organization. All of your prayers meant so very much to Keith and I both during the surgery process.

- To my expert physicians who treated me great through the whole surgery and recovery. Dr. Kristen Riley, I know what I had in you as my neurosurgeon, and never one minute was I frightened or concerned because I knew I had three great physicians looking out for me- you, Dr. Alexander Ver Hoef, and my great physician, my Father God. Thank you Dr. Ver Hoef for your brilliance in epilepsy and ability to finally figure out what was going on with my brain! Dr. Lebron Paige who was the very first doctor I saw at UAB. My life is better having known you. Dr. Scott Markle, thank you so much for being the doctor who treated me in Mobile the last time and had no idea where to go but was able to tell us that and refer me to UAB. We respected that greatly. To Dr. Hayden Long, I want to thank you for not just letting me be another patient you see. I appreciated the excitement you had for my case from the very first time I saw you in the office. I truly feel you were sent from the Lord to Mobile to be my physician. You are a very special and talented physician. Also, I kind of like getting to be your first success story!!! AND.... last but definitely not least, to my friend Jill Saenz, who was there from the very beginning for every visit, every test, etc. I know we have a friend in you and thank you for laughing with us, crying with us, and all the in between. I could not have had a better RN as my Epilepsy Coordinator.

- To all the family and friends who visited me in and out of the hospital, and prayed for me each and every day through this process. You mean a lot to Keith and I and the support was beyond anything either of us could have ever imagined. You all know who you are.

- To my precious Momma and Daddy.What can I say? I love you both. I am where I am today because you both prayed for me daily and never gave up on the Lord. Daddy, thank you so much for being with me those long hard days while I was in the hospital and rehab. I don't remember a lot, but I do know we watched a lot of " Everybody Loves Raymond" and our favorite... " The Andy Griffith Show". One day ole Barney will learn to center that badge!!! Ha!Ha!

- To my little baby girl, Emily, who is not a baby anymore. I just wanted you to know how very much I love you, how proud I am of you, and I appreciate the time you took to come and stay with me when you could, and I love the friendship we are able to have now.

- To my rock, Keith, the one person who has been there through every single bad night I had or had to come get me from work or whatever I was doing at the time when I had a seizure. Thank you for always being understanding, comforting, and encouraging through this whole 9-year process. You always said the right thing, but knew when it was not a good time to talk about something. Also, I would like to thank you for all of the hard work that you put into this project. It will never go unnoticed. God chose to bless us and we will give Him all the praise that He deserves for my healing. I love you so much!

- Last but not least I want to praise my Good, Good Father for healing me. My passion now is to share my story with as many as I can touch who need this hope from You. Send me out and use me wherever You choose to! I am ready to be your servant, Lord!

Introduction

I have suffered from epilepsy since birth. I like to say it never really bothered me as a child because I had everything or possibly even more in some cases than others. Growing up, the first experience I had that made me feel different was watching my friends get their drivers permit, then their license and experiencing the freedoms and independence of doing things they wanted when they wanted. I wasn't jealous or resentful, in fact I was happy for them but it was not easy. When you have a seizure disorder, you cannot hold a drivers license unless you have been more than six months without having a seizure. I resolved that it was my cross to bear in life so to speak, and I had to learn to accept my circumstances.

Later as a mom, it was difficult to listen to other parents complain about sitting in car line at school; I wished that I could pick my daughter up from school but I had to rely on others. (Maybe she will let me pick her up from work one day!) It was even more challenging as I looked for work. I never realized how shallow people could be. I was denied job opportunities when my medical condition was known, and I was dismissed (fired) from jobs after having had a seizure at work.

My journey with epilepsy is a path of valleys, hills, and in the end reaching the summit to see the fulfillment of God's promise of hope, which became healing.

Habakkuk 2:3 says "This vision is for a future time. It describes the end, and it will be fulfilled. If it seems slow in coming, wait patiently, for it will surely take place. It will not be delayed."(NLT)

This is the word the Lord gave to me in the Fall of 2007 after 32 years of living with epilepsy and had become a candidate for brain surgery, offering the hope for healing of my seizure disorder. A series of testing began in August of that year. It was during this time that I had the realization of what the Lord can do through hope, faith and peace which He bestowed upon me. Due to my obtainable perseverance from the Lord and the challenges I faced, victory was only possible through the support of my family and friends crying out to God on my behalf.

Then the Lord said to me, "Write my answer plainly on tablets, so that a runner can carry the correct message to others. This vision is for a future time. It describes the end, and it will be fulfilled. If it seems slow in coming, wait patiently, for it will surely take place. It will not be delayed.

-Habakkuk 2:2-3

Chapter 1

In 1975, at 5 years old, I began having seizures. They started with a very minor type of seizure known as petit-mal which is often referred to as staring spells. My pediatrician began treating these smaller seizures with medication. They displayed no visible disturbance but they eventually began to worsen. I was referred to a neurologist. The smaller seizures then developed into gran-mal seizures which included convulsions and other complications. These larger seizures often left me physically drained and took a day or longer to fully recover from. As I grew older, puberty saw an increased frequency in seizures. This proved embarrassing for a teenage girl whose life (like most) was shaped by peer pressure and the impression of friends and classmates.

I was taking an enormous amount of medication for my age.

It is no secret that teenage girls have those high school "drama" days in their life. With those times came many rough patches medically; my grades frequently suffered. Because of my health situation, my friends came to understand the rewards of teenage life which are sometimes taken for granted and that are not the same for everyone. I finished high school by the hair of my head and went on to Judson College. One year later, my seizures again became much more frequent and were almost uncontrollable. I had no other option but to withdraw from college. I loved school and this upset me greatly. This was a very disheartening time in my life as my friends were all away at school while I returned home.

I began working at a daycare where I enjoyed caring for children. A few years later, I met and then married my husband. Keith has always accepted me, loved me no matter the challenge, and has been supportive. Our daughter was born in February of 1994 and soon after my neurological state began to worsen to the astonishment of my doctors. My doctor(s) believed that as I got older it would not be unusual for my seizures to become less frequent. Leave it to me to change the odds! I continued to take a variety of medication and over the next 10 years went through changes in the dosage and types of medication; none seemed to offer better seizure control. I saw several neurologists and even returned to the original doctor I had known since first being diagnosed. (He had recently returned to practice after a time in administration at a local hospital.) Nothing changed. The greatest challenge came when my doctor suggested that my condition was in fact not epilepsy, but an emotional or psychological induced pseudo seizure. To put it bluntly, it was all in my head.

After consideration and fervent prayer, we made the decision to see a new physician. The change of my life occurred in the spring of 2007 and the blessings of God were apparent in my heart as I met with the new physician. After seeing me for three months and reviewing my 32 years of medical history he did the unthinkable. I have never had a doctor look me in the eye and tell me that he had no idea how to help me. He wasn't going to simply go through more trial and error and waste precious time in my life. What he did was offer hope! He had decided to refer me to the University of Alabama Medical Center at Birmingham (UAB) for testing and observation by their department specializing in seizure disorders. I was admitted in the fall of 2007 for EEG monitoring (an electroencephalogram). I was hoping for a true diagnosis and treatment, but the unexpected came in the opportunity of healing!

I left the hospital in a fog. The process of monitoring

meant that I had to have a seizure. I did and it was a very large one. This allowed for an accurate diagnosis and as the doctor explained to my family (I was wiped out), they were very successful at UAB in performing surgery to remove the part of the brain that was the source of my seizures. This procedure could render me seizure free. It was during this time that the Lord spoke to me and the revelation of God's abundant power fell on me. Brain surgery had become an option, and I started a three year process of testing with many highs and lows but God declared His glory through it all. Above all, my spiritual walk grew like it never had previously. As He confirmed the word in Habakkuk 2:3, I knew all things were happening for his glory. For me, the vision and hope the Lord had given to me was a blessing beyond comprehension. Knowing He had this vision, I felt like I could conquer any mountain and through faith accomplish anything. I quickly learned that "anything" does not always happen when we want it, but happens in God's perfect timing. Knowing that surgery was an option, I wanted it then, immediately. I learned the Lord does not work in my time; He always has a plan for us – His plan.

The physicians continued reviewing my case, and in the summer of 2009 they elected to try a new drug which provided better control of the gran-mal seizures. While smaller seizures still occurred daily, I went seven months before a gran-mal seizure occurred. Praise the Lord! After the travels through these difficulties over a two year period of time, a spiritual acceptance of His word had been revealed and given me confirmation of whatever method the Lord chose to bless with His healing. Brain surgery was not to be at that time, but I held to the conviction that one day it would.

I would have to say along with my marriage and the birth of our miracle daughter, this experience was one of the most beautiful and humbling of my life. My parents have always been a strong support through my childhood, adolescent and adult years. They have always displayed deep faith and never ceased in their fervent prayers for my health and healing. Often I reflected that I need to realize how fortunate I was; I had my health problems, but many struggle with terminal illness and lack the support of their family and even more distressing without the peace and grace that comes from a loving God.

As I move to the present day, the Lord has taught me always and forever a HOPE for anything, the FAITH to believe, and the PEACE that surpasses all understanding of Him. I hope to have opportunities to share with others who are walking the same paths I have traveled. I would like to share the knowledge of God, and expand on the spiritual growth I experienced through this mountain in my life. The only possessions the Lord requires of His children are knowing the love of God, the hope for a future with him, and the peace He has given all believers. "I can do all things through Christ who strengthens me." (Philippians 4:13)

Chapter 2

"Write my answer plainly on tablets..."

Habakkuk 2:2-3 tells us "Write my answer plainly on tablets, so that a runner can carry the correct message to others. This vision is for a future time. It describes the end, and it will be fulfilled. If it seems slow in coming, wait patiently, for it will surely take place. It will not be delayed."

Let's break this down phrase by phrase and walk through my journey. In the Hebrew, the word tablet is used to describe the stone tablets upon which the Ten Commandments were written. The word tablets literally means "in order that he will (or may) run the one reading it." In my journey, as I wrote in my Bible and began to compile this book with my thoughts and experience, I have in essence written on the tablets.

"So that the runner can carry the correct message to others..."

This part of the verse indicated the ability and need to share this word with others with an urgent obedience. As a follower of Christ we are commanded to share our faith in our daily lives. I am compelled to share the healing I have received as a ministry to bring glory to God and hope to those who may be searching for Hope that only God can give. As I have claimed the promise of healing in this journey there was no option but to write my experience.

"This is a vision for a future time..."

This journey of faith began during a quiet time soon after I returned home from my first visit to UAB in 2007. I had seen doctors in my home town my entire life for my seizure disorder. While the early diagnosis was epilepsy, my doctor had begun to believe (and try to convince me) that my seizures were not true epileptic seizures but were instead psychosomatic seizures. By that time, I was experiencing depression. I refused to believe that the seizures were the result of depression; I had been having seizures since my early childhood. This led to the bold step of seeking a different doctor. This was difficult because I loved and trusted my doctor, but felt that he had given up on me and nothing had been done to help me. After seeing the new doctor, the most unusual consultation that I had ever had with anyone in the medical profession resulted in this doctor having the humility and courage to tell me that my case was so unusual that he had no idea how to help me. What he then did was something that had never been done before that day, he offered me hope. He told me about a program at the University of Alabama at Birmingham (UAB). They had specialists in seizures and a program where they monitored and studied patients. He was referring me to that program so that I could have a complete and detailed evaluation with the prospect of an accurate diagnosis. Today, I am eternally grateful for a physician willing to admit that he had no clue, and then to refer me to someone that wanted to help me.

When I arrived at UAB, I was admitted to the unit of the hospital that performs seizure monitoring. About 25 electrodes were attached to my head, and I had audio and video monitoring 24 hours a day. Upon admission I was told I could be there for a week or longer. It was that same day I met an epileptologist – a neurologist that specialized in seizures. Over the course of that week, I had my medications reduced and was sleep deprived all with the goal of having me experience seizures so that they could be recorded on the EEG and the audio/video monitor. During the week I continued to have the smaller seizures that were a normal part of my everyday life. Problem was, these seizures really did not show the doctors any conclusive evidence on the EEG or monitor to help them make the diagnosis they hoped to make. Each morning, I had a visit from the doctor, his staff, and the epilepsy coordinator who managed the operations of this specific unit within the hospital. After three days and three nights of observation, the doctor indicated they could not make a diagnosis but he wanted to keep me one more night in the hopes something would be clear on the monitoring. The smaller seizures just were not giving anything of value in the testing. On Thursday night, I had one of the larger gran-mal (generalized) seizures. As was my normal experience, this seizure left me wiped out and as a precaution medication was given to help keep me sedated so I could rest. (As a result some of the next information was shared with me later as I recovered and returned home.)

I had a true diagnosis – I had epilepsy. It was then we learned why more local doctors were uncertain in their diagnosis and came to understand the inconsistent manner in which I was treated. The epileptologist said that there was no way that the seizure I had was any-thing other than an epileptic seizure. He made this di-agnosis from the video of the seizure. My local doctors had never seen any of my seizures, and they relied solely on EEG monitoring. The problem was that my seizures were more than likely originating in an area deep with-in the brain, and by the time any indication was notice-able on an EEG they had spread and distorted the EEG. Since no single point of origin was obvious on the EEG, they would not conclude that it was epilepsy. But it was epilepsy and not some psychological induced episode.

Next came the real eye opener, the doctor informed my husband and parents who were there, that I would be a candidate for surgery. We had no idea or expectation when we left home for UAB that this was even an op-tion. I was seeking a diagnosis and treatment and I was being offered healing. There was a specific process of tests including a psychological evaluation. They want-ed to make certain that any surgery would be a success and my emotional state of mind was a relevant factor in the success. The doctor was especially pleased to learn that I had recently re-enrolled in college with the goal of completing my education that had been abandoned years earlier due to my seizures. It demonstrated that I have not given up on life and had determined to pursue my goals and dreams in spite of my difficulties.

That fall, the testing began. I had an MRI (Magnetic Resonance Imaging), a MEG (Magnetoencephalo-graph), and several other tests. Each test was necessary to build the case that went before the surgery committee each month. There was a specific progression with the hope that each test would help them determine a more specific origin of the seizures. This testing was continued and even repeated over the course of several years. Now I understand why Habakkuk said that the vision was for a future time. The Lord orchestrates everything perfectly, and I know now that if I would have had surgery at that time, school might not have been an option. It was important to me to finish my education after having to drop out earlier due to my health. Also, it was early in this testing process that this specific journey of faith began.

One morning in the fall of 2007 I was spending some time reading in a daily devotional that I had been using. Not many people would go to some of the more unknown books of the Old Testament but that is where God would take me that morning. Habakkuk 2 would make a life changing impact on me that day. As I spent that time, I came to realize that this was indeed a specific word for me regarding my epilepsy and surgery that had recently become possible. The best description of my feelings that day was hopeful. Only with the passing of the next several years would I truly come to understand the complete meaning of the word revealed to me that morning.

In May of 2008 my parents gave me a new Bible for my birthday; this Bible came to be my "UAB Bible". After each trip to UAB (as well as at other times) I would record notes about my visits and continue to claim this as God's word to me for healing. These notes and statements of faith are recorded in the pages at and near Habakkuk 2. These pages have served as the tablets that Habakkuk was instructed to write for the answer. On the inside front cover, my Dad inscribed one of his favorite verses – Psalm 119:105 *"Thy word is a lamp unto my feet and a light unto my path."* Each time I used this Bible it was a source of encouragement and hope.

Chapter 3

"It describes the end and that it will be fulfilled..."

This part of the verse became more evident due to the number of obstacles that were put in my way. In verse 3, the Hebrew text expounds on the impatience of our humanity in society when we receive a word from Him. I know that my timetable was not God's timetable so with that in mind it was revealed throughout this journey that faith, trust and patience were necessary for the Lord to bestow this blessing of healing. "Only God knows the time for such events . . . the fulfillment will not miss God's scheduled time; it will not delay a moment beyond its appointed time."

I saw the doctor that I met during my first trip to UAB for over three years. His dedication to medicine was evidenced by the time he spent during our appointments and the testing process helping me to understand not only epilepsy but steps necessary to properly evaluate me for surgery. I quickly understood that you simply do not go into the brain and start working. Every test was designed to assist the surgery committee in precisely determining the origin of the seizures so that they could remove that (small) section of the brain with the goal of giving me seizure freedom.

The last test was an ictal spect; in this test a radioactive dye is injected at the earliest possible moment a seizure begins. If this dye is injected quickly enough the activity in the brain causes the dye to travel to the area of the brain where the seizure activity is occurring. You are immediately taken for a scan so that images of the brain can be made to record the "bright spots." I returned to UAB in July of 2008 for this test. The spect was attempted daily for several days, and finally a small seizure occurred and the injection was given. Unfortunately, due to the size of the seizure, and the timing this test was of little value; not what I wanted to happen.

I continued during this process to hold firmly to my word and to trust. I have come to realize that each moment of need was met with an affirmation during my quiet times. One of my notes on the tablet was from a time in Hebrews. God reminded me in Hebrews 10:23, "Let us hold tightly without wavering to the hope we affirm for God can be trusted to keep his promise (NLT)." I had to trust in his promise that the word given to me regarding healing would in fact be fulfilled as Habakkuk proclaimed.

"If it seems slow in coming.."

All of these visits and tests occurred as my life continued its normal course of work, college, family and other events of life including back surgery. I wanted the brain surgery and I wanted it as soon as possible; it just was not happening in my time. I realized then that all I could do was to hold on to the word that I had and believe. Somewhere during this time I came to proclaim along with the word from Habakkuk a reminder from the book of Mark in September 2009. Mark 11:22-24 says "Have faith in God. I tell you the truth, you can say to this mountain, May you be lifted up and thrown into the sea and it will happen. But you really must believe it will happen and have no doubt in your heart. I tell you, you can pray for anything, and if you believe that you've received it, it will be yours (NLT)." It was at this time I felt as though I was walking through a dry wilderness, but I knew that one day I would realize that promise that God had given me. Habakkuk tells us that it WILL NOT be delayed. The greatest part of this continuing journey was looking back at each milestone (some good, some difficult) and continuing to see the movement of God and the ever present comfort of the Holy Spirit as this word was revealed in the exact manner and method that Habakkuk instructed.

I returned to UAB in October of 2010 to repeat the ictal spect. My doctor hoped that we might get a better result this time. It was the same process, sitting in a hospital bed waiting on a seizure. One of the challenges of the ictal spect is the radioactive dye is only good for four hours. A new dose has to be ordered each day. In addition, a member of the medical staff sits with you the entire four hours waiting and watching hoping to be able to get the injection at the very moment of the onset of a seizure. Seconds are critical. It was the same process as before, seizures are unpredictable. Almost nothing each day, and on the third night I had a larger gran mal seizure. Things were not looking good, but on the fourth day we got a chance. I had a slightly larger (but still of the petit mal category) seizure than before. The injection was given, and I was ushered off to imaging for a brain scan.

In December 2010, we returned to UAB for a consultation with my doctor to learn of any progress with the surgery committee and to learn the specific results of the spect. I entered the clinic for my appointment with much excitement and enthusiasm. My excitement evaporated as the doctor showed me a copy of the image. He rather bluntly revealed that my scan "was lit up like a Christmas tree." The goal of the test was to determine a single spot in the brain where the seizures began; but as I already knew from the years of incomplete diagnosis my case was not the easy case. Just as was the case with the EEGs, my seizures spread so quickly at onset and as a result even in the less than five seconds it took to inject the dye my seizure had begun to spread and the resulting scan had no value. I was devastated. Tears flowed for several miles as we began our return trip home that afternoon. If Habakkuk said that it will be fulfilled, why was this happening. The doctor had just informed me that given there was no clear result from the spect, I had reached a dead end with the surgery path.

I had claimed my word continuously for three years as I went from test to test, visit to visit and new medication to new medication. Over the next two years, I continued to trust in the Lord for healing. I was willing to accept that my path might be one of better control through new and different combinations of medication if surgery was not possible. I would like to say I never gave up hope for surgery and complete healing but I had to accept that it would not happen in my time or in my way.

Perhaps the greatest test of my faith in this journey came in the spring of 2012. Without any prior indication or communication I received a letter from UAB. The epileptologist that I had come to trust so much was leaving. He had accepted a position with a university in another state. In the entire process at UAB including my surgery this was the only time they missed the standard of excellence I came to know. The letter was your basic dear John letter telling me of my doctor's leaving and a notice that I would no longer be able to be seen by a member of the UAB staff. In short, I was told to find another doctor. I was devastated.

I reached out to the coordinator in the monitoring unit that had been a part of managing my case since the first visit. She offered me hope; while I would no longer see a doctor at UAB (as I was no longer a candidate for surgery) she had a recommendation. A doctor, who had finished his medical specialization in seizures at their program at UAB, had recently moved to my home city. She believed he would be a good fit to continue treating me as he worked with the epilepsy specialists and the surgeons. Imagine the peace and comfort that came during our first consultation as my new doctor sat with me and walked me through my file showing me his finger prints along the way. He had not just trained at UAB, he had been part of the team that evaluated my case, watched the video monitoring, read the EEGs and other tests and prepared the reports that were part of my case. He was not only very familiar but was particularly excited to be a part of my continuing journey. I see clearly now that he was the God send that I believed him to be the day we met.

"Wait patiently..."

In 2008, the Lord gave me a new word to encourage me in the word I received in 2007 in Habakkuk. Hebrews 10:23 tells us, *"Let us hold tightly without wavering to the hope we affirm for God can be trusted to keep his promise."*

Habakkuk's admonition that "it will be fulfilled" was a promise to me that the Lord gave and all along this journey he continued to confirm this over and over again. Even though it may be slow in coming, it will be fulfilled. Without the peace of God, it would have been impossible to wait for the blessing that He had for me. As I look back, I see the many times I went back to the pages of my UAB Bible and thanked God for His peace and His promise as I wrote on the tablets the details of the visits, the tests and the results.

In Psalm 27:14 the Lord tells us to "wait patiently for the Lord. Be brave and courageous. Yes, wait patiently for the Lord."

It was hard at times going through rough patches such as job losses due to my disability, but I always managed to get back on my feet and continue moving forward. There were problems with medications as the dosages were increased and decreased to find the amount that was effective and that I could tolerate. There was even one medication the brought about bouts of anger, irritability and irrational behavior. They were difficult times, but I know they made me stronger. And as I look back, I can see that they were a valuable part of the process as I see the presence of God in each step.

"For it will surely take place..."

Two years went by as I continued seeing my neurologist in Mobile, and I continued to have seizures. (I lost two more jobs due to my seizure disorder, one job in 2012 and another in 2014 the latter of which was very hard.) When I returned to see the doctor in the

Spring of 2014, I asked him if I could go back to UAB to see another doctor and have my case re-evaluated. As noted before, my doctor was on my team at UAB in the earlier years and understood the hope that existed. He agreed and set up an appointment to return for a consultation with one of the epileptologists in December of that year. During my appointment at UAB, I was told of some of the new developments and possibilities that were available since my previous visits and evaluation. I left hopeful and excited with a return date for March the next year; as this would allow him to review my case in more detail and be better prepared to discuss everything with me. In our March 2015 meeting, the doctor advised me that he would again present my case to the board for their consultation and input. Not long after, I received a call from the director in the hospital unit that I had come to know quite well during this journey. They wanted me to return for a new round of monitoring (EEG and video/audio monitoring) in August. I arrived at UAB for monitoring; I was beginning to know the routine all too well. As I was getting settled into the room and wired up my coordinator friend stopped in to greet me. Believe it or not the doctor I had just starting to see had moved; my case would be assigned to the doctor that was on rotation on the floor that week. I was not exactly excited to be meeting a new physician (again) but the outcome of this new chapter was better than ever before. The details of this trip were similar to my very first experience including having me return later in the month for the psychological evaluation, MEG and MRI. During the psychological evaluation, I specifically recall being asked if I had a support system in the event they could do surgery. I was able to respond very quickly and clearly that he had no idea as I thought about my many family and friends that had encouraged me, supported me and prayed with me for this very time for so many years. In October 2015, the surgery committee met and based on my case offered me the new hope of a stereo-tactical EEG. This was one of the new options that had been shared with me the previous year. Again as before, the hope for this surgical procedure was to help pinpoint a more exact location in my brain where the seizures were beginning.

In the stereotactic EEG, my surgeon with the assis-tance of a robot drilled twelve pin holes in my skull and placed leads. Each lead had approximately twelve to fif-teen tiny electrodes on them. My surgeon had used all the previous data from the video, EEG, MEG and other tests to strategically place these twelve wires inside my brain. Once placed, I returned to the observation unit in the hospital to be monitored and wait. As with the many previous visits, we waited for seizures to occur only this time it was believed that the intracranial place-ment should give a more specific location by detecting the seizure activity before it spread to the other areas of my brain. In their words, they were hoping to see the "hot spot".

Praise the Lord!

My doctor could hardly contain his excitement as I experienced a number of the smaller petit mal seizures that had become such a normal part of my everyday life. You see, the hope was that one of the twelve probes would be near the source and that one of the fifteen electrodes would be close enough to get a reading so that we could move to the next step. What we got in sports terms was a home run. It appeared that each of the seizures recorded was consistent, and if their monitors were accurate not only was the probe going through the area of my brain that was the "hot spot", one of the electrodes was on <u>the</u> very spot. Before the probes were removed by my surgeon, the doctor was able to reverse electrical current into my brain through the specific electrode and simulate my petit mal seizures. The doctors hoped to get close, but I believe the very hand and spirit of God allowed the placement of that probe in the very spot.

We returned in January 2016 to meet with the surgeon. She had reviewed all of the data and had developed my surgery plan. I was officially offered surgery. As the probes had helped to pinpoint my hot spot, the actual resection would be more direct than the typical method. In the typical method, the craniotomy was a two-step process in which a large grid was placed on the surface of the brain and then after a seizure helped to narrow the location, the patient was taken back in almost immediately for the resection. In my case, they were certain so that resection would be the focus of the procedure. Finally, the hope and promise of my word from God was about to take place. As promised, it would be fulfilled, it would take place. This was God's plan and God's timing. Surgery was scheduled for February 10, 2016.

"It will not be delayed..."

February arrived quickly as we returned to UAB on February 9 for a final consultation and pre-op MRIs and labs. This journey was nearing completion. My support team was with me as waiting during surgery was my husband, daughter, parents, my dad's sister and family, one of our family pastor's (the crazy one), and a friend of my dad. I later learned of a few others that had recently moved to Birmingham that had stopped by to visit with those waiting and praying for me. The procedure was supposed to take only a couple of hours and there was a possibility that I could be discharged from the hospital and be home in about 4 days. The greatest lesson in the recounting of my story is that I have learned that even though God had a time and a plan, I often did not understand the direction that God was going to take in the fulfillment of that plan. Much like in 2007 when I wanted surgery, and I wanted it then, I was to learn that God had a different way, a better way – His way.

I have not mentioned before now but my procedure was officially called a left frontal-lobe awake craniotomy. Yes, *awake*. It was necessary to stimulate the areas of my brain at and around the surgery site to be certain that the (small) area to be removed would not cause any lasting issues with speech and other necessary functions. I would be under sedation but such that it could be lowered to perform the tests and then heightened when the time came to make the actual resection. While some may find it hard to believe I distinctly remember the time in surgery when things got complicated. Without getting too specific and technical, years of seizure medications had caused a thickening of the skull and an artery (or vein) had adhered to the skull and tore as the skull was opened. This trauma resulted in my need to be stabilized before the procedure could be continued and completed. I later learned that at the time those waiting were expecting word that the surgery was complete, they were being told of my set back and the preparation to complete the procedure.

When the surgery was complete, the neurologist and later the surgeon spoke with my husband and daughter. (They also confirmed to me later). They shared their continued belief that they had in fact found the spot. Normal brain tissue would have the appearance, look and feel of Jell-O. Most of my brain in fact had this characteristic. But they shared that the small area they removed did not; in fact, it was more the composition of silly putty. Even more amazing was that the tissue removed still had the mark of where the probe had pierced it in December! They in fact removed the very place that they believed was the source of my seizures.

In preparation for surgery during the initial SEEG, the consult in January and even the day before surgery, I had been made aware of the procedure and the possible side effects. I guess that in my excitement about the fulfillment of my promise, those warnings were minimized. I had been told that due to the location of the spot, I could have some short term issues with weakness in my right arm and leg. While I heard these warnings, I was expecting surgery and then to be home in just a few days. As a result of the trauma at the beginning of the procedure, I had swelling in my brain post-surgery. Apparently the swelling grew over the next several days as by the third day post-op I was no longer speaking and could not move my right arm (and hand) or move my right leg (and foot). It was as though I had had a stroke.

I later learned that as a result of the swelling in my brain, I had a seizure on the fourth day after surgery. On Valentine's Day night at approximately 9pm, I had a generalized seizure. The surgeon and neurologist were confident as they communicated with my family that it was not uncommon due to the amount of swelling post-surgery for a seizure to occur. And, this should not cause us to worry that the surgery had not been a success. I spent ten days in the monitoring unit that had become my Birmingham home during this journey. Between February 17 and 18 I began to communicate more, and by that weekend I began to see small movement in my hand and foot. I was able to stand and take a few steps on Sunday afternoon, and Monday I was evaluated and moved into the hospital's rehabilitation unit.

I would spend most of the next two weeks in rehab. Please know that rehab is a very serious and intensive process. I was awakened each morning very early, as I had to be dressed and ready by 8am. I received physical therapy, occupational therapy and speech therapy both morning and afternoon Monday through Friday and in the mornings on Saturday. (Thankfully we had Sunday off.) All I did was rehab and sleep and at the time I felt this was the most difficult and hardest thing I had ever experienced in my life. I definitely gained a new understanding for those who have been through something so traumatic that they needed this level or therapy.

While I cannot say I made the connection then, as I reflect back I have a complete understanding of the question in my psychological evaluation about having a support group as for the time I was moved from ICU to the monitoring unit through my stay in the inpatient rehab I would need someone other than the hospital staff with me as close to full time as possible. My husband, daughter and father were able to coordinate and remain with me. In addition, many in our extended support network of friends and family made the journey to simply lend an ear, give a hug, or be there during the stay. (We were also fortunate to have many friends and family in the greater Birmingham area that always seem to come by at just the right time.) We have also reflected back as between our church family, family and other channels of communication the prayers of thousands were being offered on my behalf.

Eventually the time came to return home. As the hospital staff normally do when someone is being discharged from rehab to go home, the day before, they will bring a yellow balloon to signify this experience. I was delighted to see the balloon for many reasons, and the most important being that to me it was a tangible sign that God had given me the hope I needed to heal me completely. While rehab was not complete, it was believed that it could be completed from the comfort of home. Due to the trauma during surgery and the area in which surgery was performed, it was expected that therapy would be necessary. In fact, I would need to relearn some things. What many take for granted or see as the simplest of tasks including writing, using a fork and knife, and putting on make up gradually returned over the next several months. Follow through with therapy was not easy, but necessary to recover. A mid-March 2016 visit with my surgeon brought encouraging words and her belief that within six months, there would be very few if any noticeable effects of the surgery.

Chapter 4

"Faith is the substance of things hoped for, the evidence of things not seen."

-Hebrews 11:1

This is another verse that has come to have great meaning and encouragement during this entire journey. It sits in a frame with a picture of two of the staff in the monitoring unit and me. It served as a reminder of the hope that had been received from the Habakkuk passage and helps to repeat that God's timing is not our timing and that just because you cannot see God at work in fulfilling His word, rest can be found in knowing that He is always at work in fulfilling His word. I looked often at this frame and the Word written on it believing that healing would come. Also, it had long been a dream to have a Volkswagen beetle. This was a dream since the teen years when friends were getting their license and learning to drive. Today I have my driver's license and the Volkswagen beetle is red. The last seizure was on Valentine's Day 2016 and the color red is a reminder of that day and the complete fulfillment of God's word of promise.

There have been two trips back to Birmingham for follow up appointments with the surgeon and neurologist. Our God is Jehovah Raphe – the God who heals. The first year anniversary has come and gone as a testimony of God's healing. During the visit my surgeon informed me that the law in Alabama to get a driver's license was not one year seizure free but six months.

God's timing is the key to everything. If He gives us a word, we need to claim it, be patient, have faith and hope, and allow God to reveal the details in His timing. The only thing that needs to be asked of God at that point is for the peace that passes all understanding and guards our hearts and minds. Trusting God throughout this journey was not easy. I have testified of tears and disappointment along the way when the timing was not my timing. One truth holds, I trusted God and held to the word given to me. One event during the middle of this journey helps to give a bit more clarity to the peace of mind. While waiting for an appointment (the lit up like a Christmas tree visit), another patient came up and spoke to me. His challenges and difficulties were far greater than my need. There was even a feeling of selfishness as tears flowed when he walked away. This young man needed healing more than I did. The words my husband shared with me at that moment have not been forgotten. "One day when you join your Father in Heaven you will have a perfect body, regardless of whether you are healed on this earth." This applied to the young man we met as well as me. The result of this exchange was a stronger faith and a deeper confidence in God's word and the additional encouragement of Paul in Hebrews. The peace of God that grew out of that day was the source of strength that allowed for a daily renewal of the belief that healing would come.

Conclusion

One year seizure free and counting! God is good all the time and all the time God is good. This is not new and by no means is it original to me but it is appropriate. It can be easy to allow the events of life to distract and during those distractions the enemy will seek to steal our joy. Doubt and confusion are some of the weapons he uses. There will be times when waiting on the Lord can be difficult; but know this, our God is greater and our God is faithful. In the challenges of life big or small turn to God, ask Him. Take the time to be still and know that He is God. Seek Him in His word as you ask and pray and rest on the assurance that He will answer.

The decision to change doctors in Mobile in 2007 was to have better care, maybe even a little better seizure control. God had a plan for healing that was just beginning. He provided the vision, gave a Word, filled that Word with hope and completed His work right on time.

Habakkuk 2:3 says, *"This vision is for a future time. It describes the end, and it will be fulfilled. If it seems slow in coming, wait patiently, for it will surely take place. It will not be delayed."*

Photos

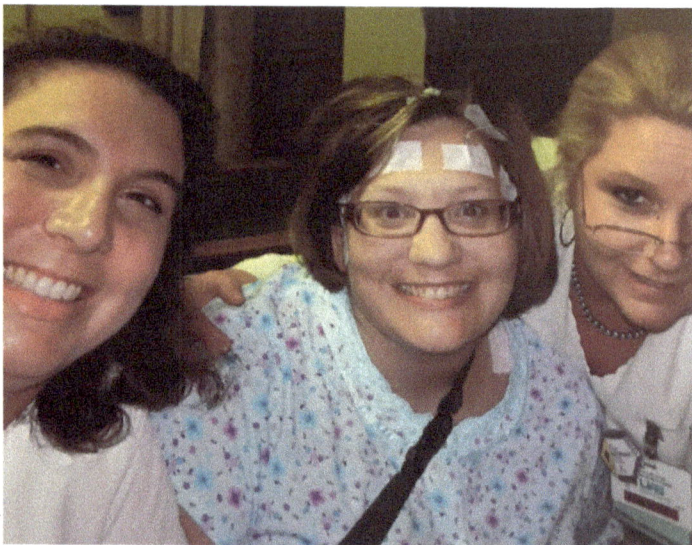

Above: Nurses Suzanne and Jill with me during 2008 ictal spect.

Right: SEEG surgery in December, 2015. My friend Heidi Alley and her husband, Paul (not pictured) came to visit when I had this surgery done.

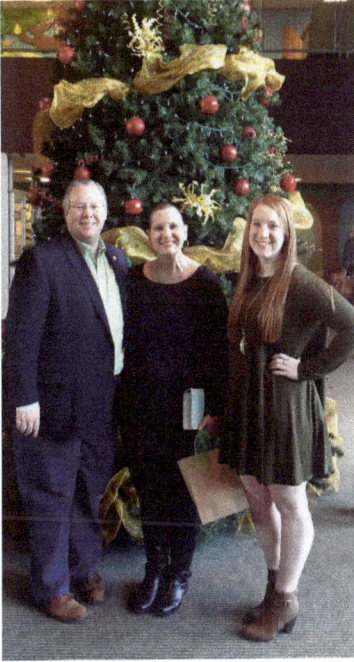

Left: Keith, me, and Emily at CHBC after my December 2015 surgery.

Right: Keith, Emily, and me with my parents, Sherman and Eleanor Williams, my Uncle Bobby, Aunt Margie, and my cousin Marcie.

Above: Me with my high school friend, Bethany Poole, between surgeries, January 2016.

Below: Between surgeries on Emily's 22nd birthday, February 2016.

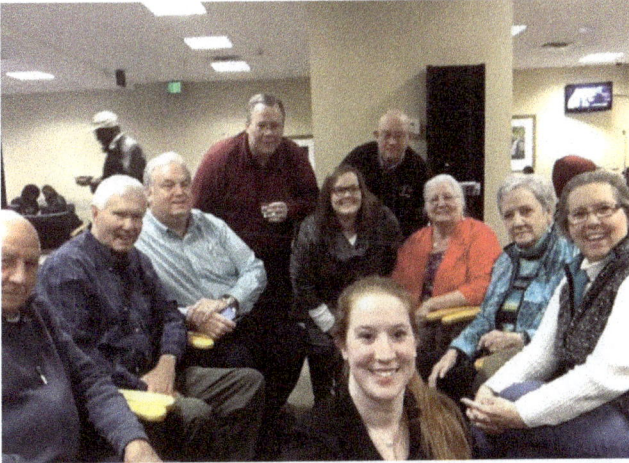

Above: The Big Day finally arrived! My cheering team in the waiting room!

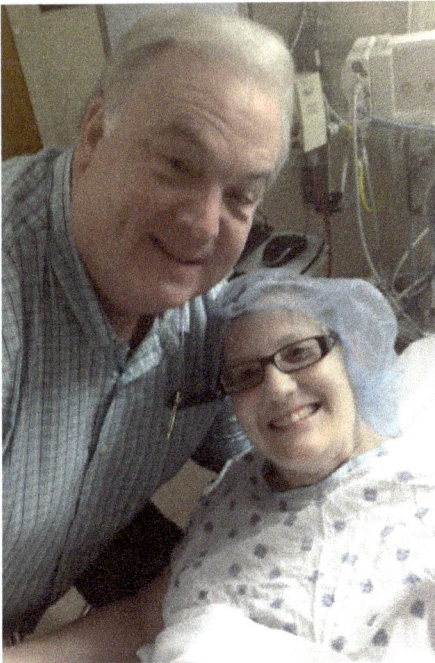

Left: Reverend Ronnie Mac and I pray before I go back.

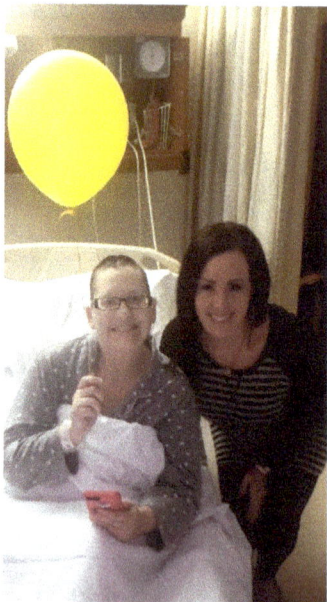

Left: My dear friend, Meredith Mc-Carson, visited me on my special day!

Right: Daddy and I, relieved we are getting to go home!

Above: Daddy, me, Emily, Keith, and Momma at Alabama Kiwanis Disctrict Convention.

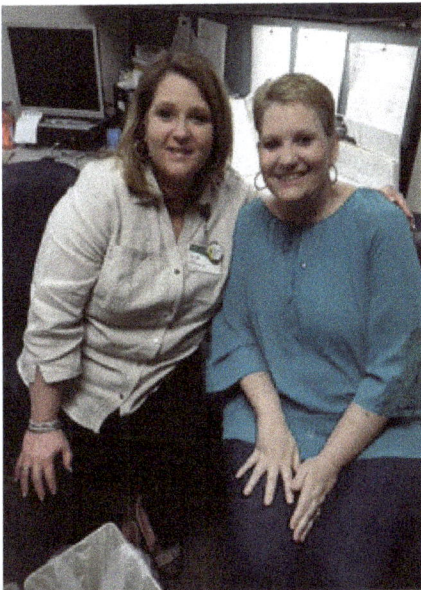

Left: Jill Saenz and I at my 6-month checkup.

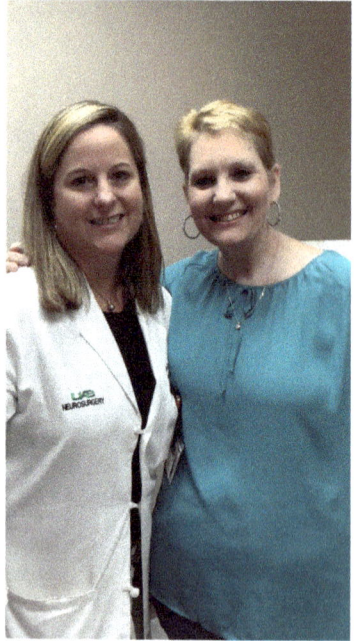

Right: Dr. Kristen Riley and I at my 6-month checkup.

Left: Dr. Lawrence VerHoef at my 6-month checkup.

Above: Keith and I taking a picture before my night out for a special "One Year Seizure Free" celebration.

Left: One year seizure free!

Above: Little did I know that when I arrived, I would have a group of very special friends waiting for me. All of these people were very much a part of my recovery and journey along the way. Left side of the table, front to back: Gwen Griffin, Gloria and Glenn Harger, Momma, me, Heidi and Paul Alley, and Ronda Ikner. Right side, front to back: Terry Plauche, Karla and Larry Moons, Keith, Emily, Daddy, Darene Bartlett, Cindy and Ronnie McCarson. It was truly a big surprise and I was speechless!

Right: Pastor Alan and I go for a ride in my bug!

Left: Dr. Hayden Long, my doctor in Mobile.

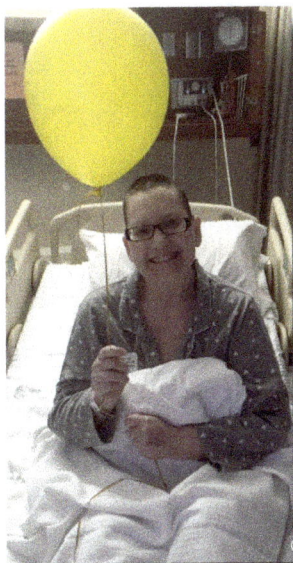

Left: Me with my yellow balloon!